PASSIVE INCOME

DO WHAT YOU WANT WHEN YOU WANT AND MAKE MONEY WHILE YOU SLEEP

BY SMART READS

Free Audiobook

As a thank you for being a Smart Reader you can choose 2 FREE audiobooks from audible.com. Simply sign up for free by visiting www.audibletrial.com/Travis to get your books.

Visit:
www.smartreads.co/freebooks
to receive Smart Reads books for FREE

Check us out on Instagram:
www.instagram.com/smart_readers
@smart_readers

ABOUT SMARTREADS

Choose Smart Reads and get smart every time. Smart Reads sorts through all the best content and condenses the most helpful information into easily digestible chunks.

We design our books to be short, easy to read and highly informative. Leaving you with maximum understanding in the least amount of time.

Smart Reads aims to accelerate the spread of quality information so we've taken the copyright off everything we publish and donate our material directly to the public domain. You can read our uncopyright below.

We believe in paying it forward and donate 5% of our net sales to **Pencils of Promise** to build schools, train teachers and support child education.

To limit our footprint and restore forests around the globe we are planting a tree for every 10 hardcover books we sell.

Thanks for choosing Smart Reads and helping us help the planet.

Sincerely,

Travis & the Smart Reads Team

TABLE OF CONTENTS

Introduction   2

Chapter 1: Active vs. Passive Income   5

Chapter 2: The How, When, and Why   9

Chapter 3: eBooks and Audios   16

Chapter 4: Passive Income through Selling   26

Chapter 5: The Real Estate Stream   43

Chapter 6: Various Income Streams   55

Smart Reads Vision   61

INTRODUCTION

Many people dream or strive to have the life they desire; to be able to resign from their 9 to 5 jobs and live a life in where they can spend more time with their families and friends, pursue other interests, travel the world, and still have financial security behind them. Unless you are one of the very few born into this plush lifestyle or come upon it because of an inheritance, then this book is a great start to helping you learn how to make extra money.

Money is not dirty or evil, as most people would have you think. Money does not bring happiness or sadness. Money is neutral, like everything. It is how we choose to use it and how we choose to live life that makes all the difference. Money doesn't bring happiness, for that is a state of being that each individual must create for him/herself. However, money certainly makes life easier and more comfortable.

The truth is, money is necessary, today more than ever. It will be extremely difficult trying to avoid using it, unless you have created a totally self-sustaining area of your own out in the wilderness somewhere. Some people like to live away from the crowds but others love the city life. It all depends on the person. No matter how you choose to live, the reality for pretty much all of us is that we need money.

In this book we will discuss how you can move away from the 9 to 5 routine forever and begin expanding your awareness in creating a passive income stream that will bring a new and better reality.

What would it be like to not worry about whether or not you are going to pay the electricity bill? What would it be like not having to worry about whether or not you'll make the mortgage or car repayments or how much will be left after you do?

Got elderly parents who might need to be moved into an aged care facility soon? Of course, you would want the best care for them. A lot of situations can catch people off guard especially those with financial consequences they aren't prepared for.

Perhaps you've wanted to travel the world or dreamed of getting a new car. Whatever it is you desire for your life, it is my intention to help you learn through this book how to set your goals and change your mindset in order to begin making the changes that will bring forth a new lifestyle. Anything is possible with the right vision, effort and time.

We will begin by assuming you know very little, or even nothing at all, about the subject of passive income. It is important to understand from the beginning that there is a bit of work involved. However, you will start to see added income accumulating passively. The work you put in initially will be well worth the rewards you will receive once your passive income starts to work for you. Passive income does not require much maintenance or management once it has been established, and money will start rolling in without you even realizing it.

CHAPTER 1: ACTIVE VS. PASSIVE INCOME

Before we begin, it's important to mention that all income, including passive income, must be declared, and the IRS still needs to receive their share since it is taxable income. There are differences in the way the IRS treats passive income, however.

If you Google passive income, *Investopedia* defines it as *"any earnings individuals receive from a rental property, a limited partnership, or involvement/endeavors where the individual is not materially involved."* The definition of passive income in popular culture, however, is slightly different – any money you earn while sitting on a beach sipping drinks. Again, before you get to this stage there is work to be done.

Three main types of income exist:

- Active Income
- Passive Income
- Portfolio Income

Active Income
This is also known as an individual's earned income. Most people have this type of income where they work or provide a particular service in return for payment. This would include salaries, wages, tips, commissions, or income from material involvement in a business. It's basically compensation from your place(s) of employment. Active income is taxed the highest. It is

also taxed to provide social security and Medicare. Most people will know that the pay they actually get after taxes is in many cases almost half of what they actually make.

Portfolio Income
This type of income hails from investments, dividends, interest, royalties and any capital gains. A portfolio income is taxed differently but is not taxed for social security or Medicare payments.

Passive Income
The easiest way to describe passive income is to say it is money earned consistently with very little to no effort on the part of the individual receiving it. Some very popular passive income methods come from interest earned, retirement earnings, or stocks. They could also be lottery winnings, online work, or capital gains. Passive income takes some time to begin working for you, unless of course, you are lucky enough to actually win the lottery.

Outsourcing Income
Go on Google and search for moneymaking activities. You will see there are many different hubs you could choose from. These are sites that promote different things on your behalf and you can sit back, relax, and watch what happens. Which one should you choose? That would be up to you once you have decided who your target audience is. The passive income you generate will depend upon whatever market you decide to go into.

Writing a blog or going for affiliate links is one way, and a very popular one at that. This will generate passive income. If you decide to write a blog, make sure you choose a particular subject to write about. It must be something you are well versed in. If you love and truly enjoy what you're writing about it will be easier to continue writing and adding more and more to your blog. The point is to continue, not only attracting, but also keeping the readers you already have. To do this they must be interested in your topic and enjoy the way you write as well.

Once you have decided you are going to become a blogger, look at which affiliate programs you can sign up to. They must relate to your topic, of course. The links to the affiliate programs should be placed on your blog posts. Some people don't go for links, however, they are a good way of making passive income. If you choose not to have links, you could have ads or appealing banners on your page.

Having and maintaining a blog is an easy and cheap way of acquiring passive income. You put in the initial effort, get yourself a core following and then you'll only need to do maintenance afterwards. You can write the blog posts alone or they could be outsourced. Just make sure you've got the ads, the banner, or the affiliate links and you should start to see an increase in the money coming in.

One other way of doing this is to think up a particular business venture, which can be outsourced to other individuals. These people could be a neighbor or an individual in another country. This particular business type could be something like web designing, marketing, programming, copywriting, or a consulting business. All of these businesses can be outsourced.

Since this seems easy and so profitable wouldn't everyone and anyone do this? The truth is that it's not that simple and the potential for mistakes is big. If you choose to go into this type of business you will need to be ambitious. You must know what it is that you want. You must know how to set clear goals and have the mental focus to achieve those goals. Achieving financial freedom by using the passive income method will require time and effort initially but once you begin to make your mark and you delegate properly through outsourcing carefully, you will soon begin to see that time and effort paying off and the life you dream of becoming a reality for you.

CHAPTER 2: THE HOW, WHEN AND WHY

One of the first things you will need to do is believe in yourself. Self-belief is a vital quality that exists in people who are happy and successful. You can be the cleverest entrepreneur or the most talented athlete but if you have little or no belief in yourself these traits will rarely, if ever, bring you success or happiness. Having a strong sense of belief in yourself does not mean you will be free of challenges. However, this belief will help you face any challenges that may arise and deal with them effectively.

"Setting goals is the first step in turning the invisible into the visible." - Tony Robbins

The next thing you need to do is proper planning. You must set achievable goals and set timelines for these goals. It's not only a matter of clear planning but also right timing. As the saying goes, slow and steady wins the race. Look over your goals. Once you start to generate passive income, what will you do with it? Would you like to invest it in a new home? A rental property? Do you want to have it in case of any unforeseen circumstances as a back up? Do you want to invest it in something else? The long-term priorities you have set for yourself will determine what goals to set. This is your why. Why do you want to generate this extra income? Many people want to get out of the rat race and resign from their 9 to 5 jobs, from rushing to work, rushing back from work etc. They want the freedom that comes with not having to rely on someone else for their income or worrying about losing their jobs. Financial freedom will bring with it more choices.

You don't have to make snap judgments or decisions like quitting your job straight away. When you are starting out in your new venture, begin gathering information, planning and setting your goals so you can start getting set up for a future you desire. Just knowing that there are so many reasons to resign from your job as well as many opportunities that are waiting could be the impetus you may need.

Starting off slowly is the way to go for most people. This will give you the time to learn how things work, but more importantly, it will allow you to mentally become accustomed to what you are doing and where you are going. Do proper research on all the options available to you and check business propositions carefully. It is important to make the distinction between slowly and steadily and outright procrastination. Be careful you don't fall into that trap. When you set clear goals, your plans, and how to execute them you'll be taking the right steps and moving in the right direction to make your dream life a reality. Don't resign from your job until and unless you are confident your new venture has really taken off and you are making enough money to maintain your current lifestyle. Don't burn bridges when you are ready to quit your job. You never know who might become a potential customer in your new start-up business.

How to Start Making Money - Proven methods of Making Passive Income

So, now we get to the how. First, think about the things that make you happy. What are you really good at? How can you serve others with this? You obviously cannot serve everyone – this could lead you down a path of failure since you can't be everything to everyone. Rather, find your niche or specialized market. Know who your target audience is and research them. The more your particular message begins to resonate with your target audience, the more opportunities you'll find to connect with them and sell.

It is best to find something you're interested in that's also evergreen or long lasting. Stay away from fads. Find something you won't tire of in the long run. If it's something already been done or is being done, don't let that stop you. Look into it further and see if you can find gaps you might be able to fill. Working out a very unique and individual selling strategy will give you advantages in any potential selling gaps. Think: What can I offer that is lacking in this particular market?

Ensure you work with integrity and transparency. This will lead to trust. Once you have established trust within your niche it will help enormously. If you fail at something, it's ok to let your audience know. Explain to them why you decided to get back up and try again. This will show resilience and this is a good trait to have. People will be able to relate to you and there will be many out there who have gone through similar experiences. It will make you more relatable and people always choose to invest in people like themselves.

Some of you may be looking for a faster track to achieving passive income. Below are some methods explaining how to do this:

The CD Ladder

A CD is a Certificate of Deposit. They generally have the highest interest rates of the government insured savings products. By building your own CD Ladder you'll be able to take advantage of both long and short-term CDs. The long-term ones are higher earning but this will mean you don't have as much access to the money as you would with short-term CDs. The short-term ones tend to have lower interest rates but you will have more frequent access to the money you've put in. Using a CD Ladder will enable you to take advantage of both options. You will be able to combine the longer-term earnings along with more regular access to some of your money.

Starting a CD Ladder is not difficult. In fact, it's quite simple. Let's look at an example: You have $30,000. You have set your goal at the 3-year mark. You could divide the $30,000 into 3 CDs evenly. Every CD will be twelve months apart and have ascending terms. Every twelve months you'll have access to a portion of the funds. Your funds will continue to mature, and this is even more important.

The ladders that are further out (year 2 and 3) have even more earning power. For this particular example we will only go out 3 years, but you'll have an option to multiply your money even more with longer-term ladders. During the one-year your CDs will grow, at the end of the 12 months you could take out your matured CD funds or "cash out." You can also choose to grow the ladder again by renewing your CD. The longer terms usually pay rates that are better. You could then continue and renew your CD into a 3-year plan, which will be purchased at the current rates. Then you repeat this particular step when you arrive at your 2nd and 3rd year maturity dates with your Certificates of Deposit. Once all the original CDs are renewed, your ladder will go into auto. They will continue to renew on their own into 3 year CDs. There will be one maturing every year until or unless you choose to stop. You will benefit from the 3-year rates and still have access to a portion of your funds that you might need annually.

Earning Higher Interest from Savings

A way to increase your passive income is to move savings to another bank that will pay you a higher rate on your savings. Sometimes little things will add up. After some time, interest rates eventually rise.

For a typical savings account, it will earn you 1/10 of a percent of the balance. This is going by Bankrate's information. The bigger banks don't generally offer higher rates. Do some research into online banks, credit unions, or even community banks if you prefer higher rates – and let's face it, who wouldn't?

Invest in Dividend Paying Stocks

Dividends are a particular way that some companies reward their shareholders for buying and owning stock. This is usually done by cash payments. Generally, companies will pay cash dividends regularly, usually quarterly. Other times they might choose to pay a one-time dividend.

A lot of people like this because they can take advantage of steady payments. You could also use it as a chance to reinvest dividends you might already have so they continue to purchase additional stock shares. A lot of dividend paying stock represents companies that have a reputation for being more mature and also have financially stable stock prices. These types of companies might steadily increase over time and their shareholders will enjoy regular dividend payments. Companies that consistently pay out are those that are financially stable and generate constant cash flow. Having stability is very important within the stocks and balances world.

Getting Cash Rebates
Many sites online use the cash rebate option. When you engage in your regular online shopping, you will earn a particular portion of your cash back on those purchases. It is often viewed as a discount, and it probably is, but there's no doubting that receiving a check that you can deposit into your bank account is a very satisfying experience indeed.

Cash Back Rewards
This is another option available if you careful about paying off credit card spending every month. Some

credit card companies offer easy income each month by using perks such as cash back bonuses. An example of its usage would be if you used the credit card to pay all household expenses every month. However, this would work only if you actually pay off the balance each month. You will be able to make some money every month just by making the necessary purchases you normally make. In some cases, credit card companies offer 8% cash rebates for any purchases. This will begin to accumulate and become easy passive income.

CHAPTER 3: EBOOKS AND AUDIO

Ebooks and audios didn't take off that well at first but have now become very popular with the average person. It is easier not having to lug around a hardback or even paperback book. Paperback books still have their place and are still loved, especially if you're not moving around too much. Devices like Kindle now allow books and audio transcripts to be easily accessible wherever people may be.

Buying books used to be a lot more difficult in terms of book covers. If a book cover isn't aesthetically pleasing, most people past it and onto another book, even if the subject matter is of interest. With eBooks and audios this is pretty much a non-issue. People will read the introduction or a short blurb and will make up their minds then and there to buy it or not. E-books are also much cheaper than hard copies so even if the book isn't to someone's satisfaction they haven't lost a huge amount of money. In addition, not having to carry heavy books is a bonus. Kindle will allow you to bring numerous books with you wherever you are going without the extra weight. You can begin to earn passive income from this type of modern technology.

Kindle
Kindle was first released on Amazon in 2007 and sold out in just a few hours. This super sell-out continued for many months until April 2008. Today, almost everyone owns a Kindle and it is a device recognized pretty much everywhere in the world. There are

different types of Kindles that people can choose from in many different price ranges.

A Kindle enables people to look through a list of titles of any type of printed material – eBooks, newspapers, magazines, and many other types of digital media files. Once people have browsed through what's available they can buy and download their choice of reading material.

Audio Creation Exchange or ACX

ACX is a marketplace for professional authors, agents, narrators, publishers and rights holders. It is a place where they can all connect and create audiobooks. If you choose to do so, after writing a book, you can narrate your own work. After all, no one knows your work better than you do. You are intimately connected to the characters, the subject, and the storyline. Making an audiobook is a very creative way for you to narrate your own story. Your thoughts and your feelings will come through directly to the listeners. Should you decide to do this and go through ACX, all your passive income, your revenue, will go directly to you. Only you will decide how your work is produced, how it's narrated, and how it's distributed.

CreateSpace
Website: http://createspace.com

CreatSpace is a self-publishing area and another option available to you. This will give you access to certain tools and also quality printing. There are thousands of people publishing works and these bring in a good amount of passive income. There is no need to chase a literary agent or a publishing company, and there is a lot of work out there that deserves to be published. People are now accessing marketing strategies and able to distribute their work like never before. CreateSpace is totally free and something that anyone can start using to take advantage of all its benefits. It provides A- Grade publishing services and will make publishing your work and its distribution very easy.

Self-Publishing
If you are a more creative person and feel you can contribute something to the world of books you might consider self-publishing an eBook. If you have something you feel you can contribute that people would be interested in, you could look into this.

You will need to find something to specialize in that will fill a gap. This will be your niche. This is your first priority if you want to make a profit from your eBook. What you will have to do is go through the best sellers at the time and find a gap, a niche you can fill. Making money through self-publishing your own book and selling it on Kindle is just the beginning. You can do more. You will need to learn how to make use of other income streams and promote your book. You can use the blog you've set up and start to develop a mailing list with all your subscribers on it. You could also give people the option of letting them leave some personal details and create another list for the other products you are offering. You could then send out any promotions you decide to run once you have your subscribers names and email addresses. You'll be able to then promote your book(s), your blog and any affiliated links. This will be discussed in more detail a little later.

Each of these income streams will begin to work together and create for you even more passive income. Once all of this is set up properly and all of the above are working together, there will be less management time for you to put in and the passive income will continue to come in.

Consider Outsourcing
Unfortunately, we are not all born with an innate ability to express or write well. Companies and individuals out there will hire others to write their thoughts and ideas. These individuals are called ghostwriters. They are the ones who actually write the books on behalf of someone else, however, their name(s) do not appear on the books or the website. All the credit will go to the company or person who hired the ghostwriter. Ghostwriters are very hardworking, talented and creative individuals, but will rarely receive any of the accolades, unless the company or individual chooses to name them, which is unusual. They are usually paid a one-off fee for writing the eBooks and do not usually receive any royalties or any other payment or recognition for their hard work, unless the company or individual chooses otherwise. They tend to work at very high standards and will go out of their way to ensure that a client gets what he/she will be paying for.

For those of you who might feel that writing and publishing a book is quite daunting, not to mention time consuming, consider hiring someone to do it for you – a ghostwriter. What you will have to do is give them a title for the book you want them to write, and also some of the things you would like included in it. You must also specify the length you'd like this book to be.

A ghostwriting employment schedule can be a shorter or a longer schedule. It's entirely up to you. It is possible to use a ghostwriter to write several books without even having to meet or speak to the person. It can all be done online. That's where the term ghostwriter comes from – the person is essentially a ghost. Ghostwriters exist at every talent level and demand levels. You will choose who you feel is more appropriate to work with. The payment details are also up to you. Ghostwriters will usually make only pennies in the dollar.

Should you choose to outsource writing a book and use a ghostwriter there will be some upfront costs. However, considering an average thirty-page eBook takes around one to two weeks to write and the income will continue to come in once it's out there, your money will be well spent.

Keywords
Once you've decided on your subject, written your book or chosen a good ghostwriter to do it for you, and have a very well-written eBook, you will need to start thinking about some of the keywords that

basically describe what readers can find in your book. It is the keywords that will enable readers to find and know your book(s) exist.

Think carefully about the keywords you will use as they have potential to crack a totally new market for you. It might lead to an increase in foot traffic (so to speak) coming onto your product page. This will lead to potential customers finding out that your book or eBook is available. It stands to reason that, if people don't know about your product, they won't buy it. Becoming more familiar with keywords will help you become a more successful and effective self-publisher.

The keywords are either words or phrases and target words that will help your book rank higher online when a person puts those words into their search. There is a fine line you must adhere to in order to be more successful in this area. Choose something generic to bring the type of traffic you need, but do not be vague either. If you've written a book on philosophy you don't want the people searching for computer programming coming to your site.

There are certain words that will get more traffic than others. There are also some popular keywords which get much less competition. It will be wise to use such keywords. On Amazon you may use up to seven keywords before you upload your book. It is these words that will assist Amazon to work out the algorithm and work out where your product will show on the results list.

There are also SEO or Search Engine Optimization keywords that are more universal. The SEO keywords are important. These will not only go through Amazon's search engine but out into Google and Yahoo and other search engines. This will help drive more of the outside traffic towards your product page. The difference between Amazon's keywords and SEO keywords is you do not officially select them. What you'll need to do is identify the SEO keywords you need and start using them strategically on your product page. You might even decide to insert these particular keywords into the title of your book. You may place them in the subtitle, the introduction, or perhaps the summary.

Final Steps to Becoming a Self-Publisher
You are now getting closer to becoming a fully self-published eBook writer. With this will come another goal you have set to achieving and maintaining a passive income using this means. Using CreateSpace will mean you must first sign up and get your own account. You will create a new title, and this will take you to the beginning of a new project page. When you are there you'll fill in the relevant information regarding your eBook. When you are ready to choose a cover for your book CreateSpace has this covered too, making it a very useful tool indeed. CreateSpace will take you through every step and help you along the way. You will be prompted to choose a book cover once the book has been successfully uploaded. At this point you will review your eBook, choose distribution channels, set it at a competitive pricing and then write a description – make sure you keep it short but

relevant. At this stage you will have successfully self-published your very first eBook. If you would like to do this again you will then have the knowledge.

If you decide to use the Kindle selection you should upload your book at this point. Kindle has its own direct publishing area. Many people feel overwhelmed when they first see all the instructions. However, if you have a closer look you will see that the steps are not that complicated. In fact, it's quite a simple process:

• You log in by using your own Amazon account.
• Enter the personal information requested.
• Start the process and upload your content.
• Publishing takes around 5 minutes (or less!) Within 24-48 hours you will have your very own eBook available on the Kindle site worldwide.
• Relax, and watch as your passive income grows.

ACX for Audiobooks
Website: http://www.acx.com/

For some people, going the audiobook route is preferable to the eBook route. We briefly mentioned ACX above and now will explain a bit more about it here.

ACX has production rates that are quite low. This means more of the passive income goes directly to you. ACX is a site that manages audiobooks.

If you're not so keen on going the eBook route then you might want to try audiobooks. ACX has lower production rates. This will mean more passive income coming to you. ACX manages audiobooks through Amazon, Audible, and iTunes. All of these sites have proven themselves as industry leaders. If you use ACX you will also be offered the choice to be the narrator for your own book, or to hire someone else to do it for you. You will need to speak everything from your book, including the title, the book description or summary, and then the actual story or text into the audiobook. As mentioned before, someone else could be hired to do this for you if you don't want to or don't feel comfortable doing it yourself.

If you decide to hire someone as a narrator, take a chosen portion of your book and use it as a script for when you audition the potential narrators. When you have chosen the narrator you will have to find someone to produce it. Once again you can use a particular part of the book to use in the audition for the role of producer. Review the candidates and then make one of them an offer. If a producer decides to accept your offer then you will have officially made a deal on ACX.

The producer you choose will then record a fifteen-minute checkpoint. It is here that you'll have the chance to give some feedback and your approval (or not) of the process up to this point. Once you have approved the sample, the producer will continue to record until he/she has completed the process. When it's complete and you're satisfied with the services, you'll pay the producer and are ready to distribute the audiobook. If you choose to, you could also pay the producer in royalties. Either way, it's up to you and your producer how you prefer to work out the payments. With your audiobook completed, passive income will not start to grow.

The next thing is to market your book and maintain positive reviews. You should consider hiring a VA – virtual assistant, who will help you do this. A VA will be able to help you with any part of the workload. He/she can gather reviews for your book and help with the marketing. Your VA can also complete research you may need or contact some bloggers to help you promote your book. The VA could also write an honest review for you online. He/she could help you set up distribution lists where you could send the book and receive feedback or other reviews. Hiring a VA is a good idea, as it will give you more time to explore other opportunities of making passive income.

CHAPTER 4: PASSIVE INCOME THROUGH SELLING

In this chapter there is much crucial information and it would be wise to make the time to read it carefully. This is a long chapter but necessary. Part of achieving passive income is having the opportunity to market or sell something you know. Several ways of doing this are mentioned below.

We will start by discussing Amazon, which is in fact the biggest online retailer in the world. This is based on total sales and market capitalization. Amazon HQ is in Seattle. Amazon is a success story in itself. It began as an internet bookstore then went on to sell audiobooks, DVDs, video games and other electronics, home furnishings, and apparel. It is now known as a very convenient place to shop for almost anything.

FBA - Fulfillment by Amazon
Website:
https://services.amazon.com/fulfillment-by-amazon/benefits.htm

FBA is something offered by Amazon whereby customers are able to store products through the Amazon fulfillment center. Amazon does the manual work for you. They pick out products for you, pack then and ship them and also provide customer service with regards to the products. Amazon can and will boost sales for you using their tools and the manpower they have. This will supply your orders on demand.

Before setting up your Amazon sellers account you must find and also manufacture a lucrative product. It is totally up to you how much you choose or can invest initially. Do your research carefully to ensure you buy and sell the right types of products at the right prices and you should easily begin to make sales and profit fairly quickly.

Once your product is ready to market and you are producing goods, it will be time for setting up your sellers account. Create product listings and add them to the Amazon catalogue. You can add your products one by one or you could do it in bulk. You must ensure that any products you want to sell are well made and prepared so they can be safely shipped anywhere in the world and go directly to your customers.

The next step is to create some shipping plans. It's a good idea to use a carrier plan that's discounted. Amazon is partners with UPS and offer huge discounts. The costs are billed to you so it's in your interests to make sure you can get as big a discount as possible. Amazon also has sellers' tools that assist you with queries or questions so it will not be as daunting an experience as it may sound.

Now you must start dealing with actually making money. Customers can now order the products you sell online. Customers who are members of Amazon Prime receive fast and free shipping for your products.

For customers who aren't prime members Amazon has free shipping on certain eligible orders. Amazon works very quickly and efficiently to fill orders and customers receive Amazon tracking information so they know at what stage their order is at any given moment.

One last thing that Amazon provides, and it's a great service, is that it will provide customer support for any product you sell. Their teams offer A-Grade service on questions, refunds, inquiries, returns, and feedback 24 hours, every day of the year.

Amazon opens up great opportunities for anyone to be able to benefit from passive income. All you have to do is make sure the products you produce are well made and sought after and Amazon will do the rest.

Informational Products & Online Courses

People are actually making a decent living through successful informational businesses. In fact, there are quite a few product businesses today. Perhaps after reading this you might come up with your own ideas and begin to make even more passive income.

Online courses are good ways of making passive income. If you can create a certain online course, you can teach something one time and get paid for it again and again. In some cases, these online courses are viewed as more valuable than an eBook. You are able to set up daily or weekly distribution lists and can have a higher product turnover than the eBook process. Generally, people check their email more than once or twice a day. If you send out courses through a listserv (an application which delivers messages to subscribers on an electronic mailing list) then you will more likely remain relevant and connect with people who can use your courses. This will help your passive income grow. If your courses are useful people will continue subscribing. Word of mouth is effective and they might recommend you to family or friends. People who are satisfied with a product usually share their experiences with others. The same goes for people who aren't satisfied with a product so make sure it is well made and you are transparent.

YouTube
Website: Youtube.com
 Perhaps eBooks and online courses are too serious to be considered by you. Perhaps you prefer something a little different. If so, you might choose to get a YouTube program going. It is not only for younger kids anymore. It has become a very relevant source for tutorials and also ecommerce. It is actually now one of the top search engines used for finding fix-it solutions or DIY projects.

A recent study showed people watch YouTube for 6 billion hours each month! This is an enormous amount of time for people to be online watching anything. For you, this could develop into many viewers who can bring with them opportunities and a lot of business. This is another online marketing instrument and you can have branding and also traffic literally at your fingertips.

Setting up a YouTube channel of your own is not difficult. You can begin with just a small video recorder or a webcam. When you become more experienced you may start using a more advanced digital camera, perhaps even a high definition camcorder. You should also get yourself a proper microphone. People have to be able to hear you clearly and hear what you're selling. It will also have a very positive impact on the video quality. Looking like you've just made a quick shot in your basement will not help you or your product to be taken very seriously. Good quality microphones exist for all types of budgets. You must also make sure the camera you're shooting from is stable. Use a tripod to make sure your video is smooth, not bumping everywhere.

Another thing you might want to invest in is simple lighting to void overhead shadows. Most conventional lighting looks cheap and allows shadows. This won't benefit you if you're trying to make a good quality video. You might decide to mix some different colored fabric for different backgrounds to create character or ambiance. Support stands from photography backgrounds are not too expensive and will likely pay off by giving you a more professional look in your video.

Aim the camera correctly, shoot and record. This is what you need to do to sell your product or tutorial on YouTube. Editing software might come in handy too; nothing fancy or expensive, after all, you just need to make minor edits.

When you have a channel running, you must decide exactly what type of product or type of tutorial you want to sell. You might want to add more videos such as a Q & A section. It is likely customers will have questions before buying or after buying. The Q & A section has the potential to boost sales if it helps someone who is hesitant to actually purchase something. Putting the question and answer section there before people need to ask will also show you are proactive. More importantly, this section will save you from having to answer the same or similar questions every day.

You could also have a few behind-the-scenes video clips on your YouTube channel. People tend to like these and they do well, in particular with branding. If you actually make the product yourself it might be worth your while to show how the process works from your end. It will help give viewers some faith they're buying real quality products.

You might decide to focus on topical content that will help your viewers figure out solutions to problems. Topical content can get through to thousands more people, whatever you think might keep your customers further engaged and keep coming back. If, for example, you sell clothing, you can show subscribers how to pack a suitcase properly when they've got a lot of things to put in there, or perhaps a must-have list of things they can pack for specific types of vacations.

If you can get some honest feedback and some great reviews it will help you along. How do customers use your product? Do they like the product? You might want to interview some of the customers who are willing to do this and after getting their permission you could share their interviews and stories on your YouTube channel.

Now, the next thing you should think about is how you can generate traffic to your own YouTube channel. Well, YouTube has several ways viewers can interact.

1. Annotations – this is the best way to market on YouTube. They can be used as call-to-action posts at specific places in your video: at the beginning, the middle and the end of your video are good places. You will be able to link these to other videos on your particular channel.

2. Video descriptions can lead to more clicks and more leads. They are sometimes overlooked. However, they are good to have and include links to your page and a description of your own video. Use keywords for this too.

3. Promoting your channel by engaging your viewers. Make sure your Q & A page is well set up and engaging the viewers. Answer some of the comments to your video. Don't be too aggressive in promoting your video when you are on other video comments pages. Be subtle and be helpful and the selling will start to happen.

4. Use means outside YouTube to endorse your channel. Message friends who can promote your

channel and generate more views by connecting relevant newspapers or bloggers to share your videos.

5. Share or post about your channel on invoices you send out or on shipping information that goes out with orders.

6. Promoting within YouTube itself can be done by creating a segment and asking people to subscribe to your channel. Insert a phrase or segment towards the end of your videos with an annotation that points to your subscribe button. Use a brand image in your channel header. Put all the details in the "About" segment with clear information about your particular brand.

If you want to sell on YouTube you will need to put in time commitment. If you take enough time to create your own YouTube channel and successfully run it, it will open up more opportunities that can help you to implement, sell, and also further advertise your products.

Stock Photos
What are stock photos? These are images that have been taken by someone then licensed to be available for use in various ways. So with this again, you can do something only one time and it can continue to make passive income for you. For a magazine cover, for example, a photographer will take very specific pictures for articles in the magazine, perhaps a model wearing a particular brand of clothing for a women's wear feature. A stock photo is the opposite of this. If

you take a beautiful photo of the beach at sunset or the desert at sunrise, perhaps on your travels, and you could upload it to stock photo houses. These are brokers who have clients looking for certain pictures. Your photo might be bought for use one time or many times over.

Photography could be a hobby or a job, or another passive income stream. What you must do if you are thinking of going down this route is to understand and figure out what it is people are actually looking for. Then you will have an idea of what is required to capitalize on this niche.

It's not difficult, in fact it's very easy, to take a photo and sell it as a stock photo which might contribute to websites, brochures, or product advertisements. So many of these photos are actually taken by everyday people going about their lives and not necessarily by professional photographers.

Both stock house and photographer (you) will receive some money every time clients use your image. How much money you make will depend on the price you negotiate and the fees of the stock house. Again, passive income means you can be bringing in money anytime of the night or day. Your photo can be accessed anytime by anyone once it has been uploaded to a stock house. Good quality photos that are clear tend to sell well. Make sure the photos you send to the stock house are not blurry or out of focus. Create a selection of photos that people or organizations can choose from and make money even while you sleep. The possibilities regarding stock photos are endless.

Make sure you research and find reputable stockbrokers to choose from when you decide to distribute your photos. A good broker should be able to provide you with good information about what their particular clients are looking for. They can help you work out what will make your photos better and also perhaps help you with any technical questions you may have.

When choosing a stock house do your homework first and compare terms and also payout rates. You might choose to sign up and be an exclusive distributor with only one broker. This might hinder overall income, however. You might decide to distribute your photos on several sites and this would generally be more valuable as your work will be distributed further using different channels.

*Note: Not all pictures you send in will be accepted. Don't take it personally if one or more of your photos is rejected. Stock houses have to make money too therefore they must make sure only the highest quality photos are presented to their clients. Try to work out what are the useful aspects of stock photos from the client's perspective. Just because you think your photo is fantastic it doesn't mean the client thinks so or can use it.

In addition, make sure you read copyright agreements. Individual stock houses have different terms. Read these terms before signing up or agreeing to anything. Understand your rights when it comes to attaining the photos. In some cases, you will have no rights at all once the photos are handed over. Avoid contracts whereby you cannot use photos you yourself have taken because the terms you agreed to deny you this right. Understand all legalities before signing or committing yourself to anything.

One more thing to consider when sending in photographs is that your photo will be used for whatever the client deems necessary. For example, a photo you have taken might be used to warn people of the dangers of sexually transmitted diseases or for a domestic violence campaign. If you want to avoid this you can stick to more generic content such as natural landscapes. This way there should be no problems in the ways your photos are used.

Drop Shipping – What is it?
Drop shipping is a method of providing goods by direct delivery from a manufacturer to a customer or retailer. It is really one of the easiest ways to sell online. It basically cuts out the middleman. Drop shipping is a type of retail fulfillment method whereby you purchase products individually from wholesalers and ship them directly to customers. People everywhere use drop shipping to move product. The two most popular sites are Shopify and eBay.

With this method, retailers don't keep goods in stock. Using this model you find a supplier to work with and list all the merchandise they have for sale. When an order comes through you will send it on to the supplier where it is fulfilled. The supplier will then ship the products from their warehouses, where they pay for the space, the workers, the electricity etc. and it goes out to your customers. It is something like what Amazon does. The difference with the drop shipping method is it is not necessary to invest a lot of money to buy inventory. You only buy something when an order comes in for it.

Not having to buy every single product you sell and keep it in stock somewhere allows you to offer more products to customers. This type of online store greatly reduces risks associated with other business models. If you had to buy everything up front and it didn't sell you would be left not only with a significant amount of stock but also very much out of pocket. This way stress is also reduced as you don't run this risk or have to manage a warehouse full of inventory. All you need is a reliable computer and reliable Internet access.

Drop shipping can be quite a profitable business. Of course, as with everything, you will need to put in the effort, the energy and the time. You'll need to have commitment and dedication. However, if you are willing to put these all into practice it is a business that comes with very little risk and can pay off big time in terms of passive income. If you find a particular niche that works well you can start making a profit. Prepare yourself mentally for the hard work and dedication that will come when you are first starting your business. Once it is established it can operate for the most part without you having to do very much at all.

Shopify
This is common among many ecommerce businesses and also an answer to drop shipping. You have to set up your own online store and sell products. With Shopify it is possible to organize items and also customize your own storefront too. It is a site set up which can take a credit card payment from you. You can also track orders and respond to them using only a few mouse clicks. Considering it is web-based and is ecommerce software you will not have anything you need to install. Shopify works and it is compatible with many other operating systems. All guesswork of how to run an online store is taken out completely. You will set up and prepare your storefront. Then begin to generate some revenue. Shopify offers a 14 day free trial to allow you to become accustomed to the way it works. Once the trial period is over and you have decided to work with Shopify, you will be offered a wide variety of pricing plans from which to choose. Look at them carefully and choose the ones that best suit the size of your particular business and your nature.

eBay
Another very popular marketplace online that has become huge in buying and selling is eBay. Anywhere in the world, people can connect and buy goods or sell them. The way it works is thus: a seller will list an item on the site. It could be anything – books, furniture, coins, cars, even houses. You name it; you can find it

on eBay. The seller can choose to allow bidding (like in an auction), or opt for the buy now process. If the seller chooses the buy now option buyers will have the chance to buy immediately at a fixed price that is set by the seller. With this option there is no negotiating.

The bidding process, or the auction, (bidding) will usually open at low prices. Sellers will determine how long the bidding will continue at the beginning. Buyers who are interested will bid against one another for certain items. When the bidding time is over and the listing has expired, the buyer who bid the highest will get the item. Selling and buying this way is not difficult and for those who prefer a challenge it can be lots of fun too.

On sites such as eBay and Shopify drop shipping is a good way to make some passive income.

Affiliate Marketing
Affiliate marketing is another passive income stream you can look into, especially if you feel you cannot come up with a product that can generate enough sales. It is also another thing to do for those who want to expand their passive income streams. Affiliate marketing is based on earning a commission by promoting other people's products. With this you can also promote some business products too. People seem to find it easy to promote things they like therefore this could perhaps be the first step. So, find products you like and promote them. Then you can earn a part of the profits, which will be based on every sale you make.

Affiliate marketing requires little skill but there are a few tricks and tips you must know about that will make it easier for you. First of all, it is about relationships. If a person you know recommends something to you, really listen to them and what they're saying. Listen carefully to keywords they use. Make sure you are sincere with what you are doing, in particular with your online activities. This will form the basis of effective skills in affiliate marketing.

The tools mentioned above can be great resources when it comes to affiliate marketing. Try focusing on bringing more traffic to your site. More traffic will potentially mean more people looking at and perhaps buying what you're promoting. If you're already using a particular product then promote that thing first. For example, if you happen to be using a specialized type of lighting to make your videos for your YouTube channel, you could begin promoting that first. Become more aware of what you do and what is around you that you use and begin with those products.

The best thing you can do is promote products wisely, without excess or undue flattery and without being afraid to be honest, but don't be too blunt, use a bit of diplomacy. Negativity is not necessary. Just cover the facts. Discuss what worked with the product and what might be improved. Remember: trustworthiness is essential and in the long term it will pay off. One thing you might want to do if you feel a product is not living up to its potential is to contact the particular company before you put up a review and tell them what you think about their product, again being diplomatic and just sticking to the facts without insulting anyone. They might be able to improve on their product and your review might be different.

The wisest products and the ones that tend to sell the best are those that help people solve problems or perhaps help them with some of their fears. These types of products are good because people don't lean towards buying things they don't know much about. People who feel more comfortable and can understand something a little better are more likely to buy it. Knowing your audience is important, and as discussed earlier in this book, do some research to find out who your target audience is and what they want. To give an example, if people who follow you are outdoorsy types then it would be silly to be promoting indoor activities on your site.

Another tip you must learn is knowing how much your audience will spend. If the people who follow you don't have much disposable income then they will likely be interested in buying products that are not very expensive.

Now let's discuss the holiday season. Again, this comes back to what type of audience you have. If they go on vacation around the holidays then they most likely won't be taking their computers with them. Promoting around this time may be a waste of time and effort. Perhaps they are they looking for the best deals around this time? Then you must promote and promote well during the holidays. Knowing your target market is imperative because when you know them you will have information on what to promote, when and for how much.

Your VA, if you choose to have one, could also help you do affiliated marketing on your eBooks or audio. Of course, the VA will need to get some of the profit for this, however, the work they do will help increase your sales which will result in more money and more time for you to pursue further passive income ideas.

CHAPTER 5: THE REAL ESTATE STREAM

Many people might not think real estate has any connection to passive income, however, you will see that in fact, they have something in common.

Real estate is one of the few investment streams that have made many people wealthy. Property or land investment seems to have remained a constant in investment history. Is it really a passive income stream or is it a myth?

You can invest in property real estate in two different ways: direct and indirect purchases. A direct purchase will involve a larger upfront cost but it will potentially yield higher returns. An indirect investment is usually made through a real estate investment trust, (or REIT), or tax liens, which is the right to keep a property which belongs to someone else until any taxes owed have been fully paid. Therefore, using the indirect route you will not have direct or immediate possession of a property. We will discuss both these methods in more detail below.

If you choose the direct option you will need a down payment in order to purchase the property in the first place. This could be anywhere from 10 to 30% of the cost of the property. You can see this would be a large chunk of money to pay out but as mentioned before the investment returns would be much higher. You will then need to lease the property at an appropriate price. You may want to do this through a real estate agent and have them manage the property. They would collect the rent, chase it up if it's late, deal with any issues such as a leaky faucet or electrical problem etc. Of course, this would eat into the money you would collect each month, however, not that much considering they would be fully responsible for the everyday running of the property.

Another very important thing to consider is where you will buy your rental property. Some people have done well buying in lower socio-economic neighborhoods while others have found they make a loss because of unpaid rent and major repairs they have to make. Choose carefully. Joseph Hogue, CFA, advises never buying in a neighborhood you wouldn't want to live yourself because if anything goes wrong and your business fails for some reason, you might have to live in one of the houses you've invested in. This is just something to think about.

In this chapter we will discuss rentals to achieve passive income. There are other passive income streams that can be made from real estate such as "flipping"- buying a property and remodeling it to sell at a much higher price and make a profit this way. The flipping option will require much more work as well as higher funds.

The potential to make income and how much of it you will make depends on many different possibilities and how you choose the method or strategy you use. You must know exactly how much money you are willing or are able to spend. You must also understand yourself enough to know if real estate investment is a project you can take on and see it through. It is important to know what jobs you can do on your own and what jobs you will have to hire others to do. This will take some of your immediate cash flow right at the start, but on the other side it will move you even closer to achieving a passive income.

Research the real estate business so you know what you're getting into. Going blind into any situation is not a good idea. You must decide if you want to buy and rent out commercial properties or residential ones. With the commercial properties such as those for offices and other businesses, the returns are usually lower but they may also have less management issues in the future. Commercial properties generally cost more to purchase,
If you choose to go down the residential property real estate market remember what I mentioned before – choose a property in an area you wouldn't mind living in yourself. In lower income areas you can buy and fix the house then rent it for more than it originally was. However, the drawback here is you will likely have a high turnover of tenants from year to year. If you choose the higher income area you will have more stability with regards to tenants but you'll have higher monthly payments to make.

Start this venture off small. Look around and find an apartment or house you can see yourself and your family comfortably living in. It's better if the place doesn't need much maintenance and repairs. Make sure any repairs you need to do are things you are ok to do. Look for updates that you can cosmetically make at first. Things like new carpeting or fresh coats of paint will instantly transform a house and make it look better and more marketable. The average person can do this on their own and this means less money coming from your pocket.

When you have become a little more experienced and know what to look out for when investing in real estate you can use this information to move to other options and get your business financed properly.

Financing Real Estate Investments
Very few people can pay cash to get a property. Another positive, apart from passive income through real estate, is being able to buy properties using borrowed money. You can then write off the interest you pay on taxes as business expenses. Often, new investors take out conventional mortgages to buy their first property. They will use a 10-30 percent down payment. A higher down payment will decrease monthly payments and increase your cash flow. It will likely reduce returns on money you originally put up, however.

If you have a good credit score rating you will be able to get a normal mortgage but the interest rates may be higher on a rental property than a loan on owner occupied homes. For those who cannot get a loan that will enable them to pay the mortgage, there are still other options available. The rates will likely be much higher, however. One option is personally approaching the seller. They might be willing to sell or perhaps finance the property using monthly installments. Another option is having a partner to help finance the money. The second option isn't always possible for a new investor who has little experience but perhaps it might be another option in the future. When you have a bigger portfolio it might be an option to think about because it will be a bit easier working with other people that you've built a relationship with while you were working on this business project. Money partners often lend money based on a particular rate or by getting a percentage of the profit. They might even choose to do both of these, as long as it is acceptable to you. Just be very careful with any partner and make sure the person is trustworthy and works with integrity.

Locating a Property
There are many different ways people can go about finding a property to help their investments grow. Multiple Listing Services (MLS) are very popular and widely used by people including real estate agents themselves. Through these services you can search for very specific requirements. You may decide to explore and build relationships with real estate agents and they might be able to give you good leads on potential properties that are for sale and would suit you.

You must be very clear and know exactly what you want when discussing this with an agent. If they are very good at their job they will be very selective in what they show you. You must be sure you're looking at a good, solid house and not just a really good deal. In some cases, cheap houses could be money pits in the near future for you, so do your own research before buying.

You could also check the REO pages of banks. REO stands for real estate owned and are houses that have been foreclosed and which banks own. These are often good value because prices for these places are listed on banks' pages. In some cases, you might even be able to negotiate a better price than what's on the REO list.

Sheriff sale properties are another option you could look at. These are properties usually managed by the country sheriff's or treasurer's offices. Usually these places have a judgment against them like a foreclosure notice that goes before a bank's REO comes out.

Perhaps this type of search is too complicated for you and you prefer something simpler. If that's the case then you could search for properties that aren't for sale but are abandoned or a little run down. This will take you more legwork but you could find a really good deal and not have to deal with any competition or hassles from other buyers or investors. Once you have the address you go to the county's assessor website and get the owner's details. This is a site that will also give you loads of other information such as property value, previous sales information, house measurements, and other characteristics. You must find out the price to know if it is right.

There are two popular ways of valuing a property:
- Comparable sales information

- Capitalization rates

1.) Comparable Sales

This involves valuing a property against other similar properties within the same area that has been sold recently. Write down what characteristics this property has, such as when it was built, square footage, how many bedrooms and bathrooms, and the kind of neighborhood it's in. Also note specific features such as air-conditioning, a garage, a completed basement etc. Compare these specifics with the other properties' specifics and features and then you can better compare the prices. Compare around 10 sales to give you a proper idea about average values for targeted properties. This is a simple process as long as your county's assessor is up to date.

It is easier to compare properties if you set a particular range for the search. Most places are different in square footage and features so look for houses built around 10-15 years of one another and a difference of only few hundred feet of square footage. Try to compare houses, which are as close as possible in their characteristics.

When you've got a list to compare and work from, divide selling prices by square footage and this way you can find out each house's price per square footage. When you've got an average price per each square foot then you can write them down from the most to the least expensive. This way you will be able to work out target values of the properties you are looking at.

2.) Capitalization Rate

With the capitalization rate you might not get as accurate a market value rate but it's indeed more straightforward. The capitalization rate is basically the annual net operating income, or NOI. To calculate this you must take the capitalization rate of your house and divide it by the cost or the value. The net operating income will be any monies left over after all other expenses have been paid.

For example, you've purchased a property with the intention of renting it out at $750 per month. 720 x 12 (months) = $9000. Now subtract any operating expenses from the gross income of $9000. This might look something like this:

Property Management - $900
Maintenance - $450
Taxes - $710
Insurance - $650
= $6290   left as your net income.

Then you can calculate the capitalization rate by dividing the net income from the purchase price.
Example:
$6290 divided by $40,000 (purchase price) = 0.157 = 15.7% cap rate.

Some might think it's a lot of work but figuring out the approximate value of a property is essential to figuring out if you're getting a good deal. Don't be afraid to haggle or negotiate a lower price if you can.

Don't allow yourself to be rushed into anything and then find out you've been ripped off and paid way too much for a property that isn't worth it. Enter any negotiation with a maximum price in mind and also a starting offer. From there, move on to other options and try to move towards a final price.

Tenants

You can post online. Your online selling methods will now come into play. You will be able to generate many views using the online skills you have learned. Many search engines exists in which you can place an ad for tenants and the sites are usually quite cheap to use and give people the ease of shopping in the comfort of their homes.

When you have a potential tenant or tenants you must vet them carefully. It is better to do the initial legwork rather than putting anyone in your rental property and then have problems with them throughout their entire lease period. They may trash the property and cost you money in missing rent or eviction fees. Perhaps you could even drive past the tenants' current property and have a look to see how they are maintaining that one. Interview and run checks on potential tenants. Do a criminal background and credit checks. These will not always guarantee a problem-free tenancy but it is the best that anyone (including real estate agents) can do. Once you have chosen the tenants you should go through any rules you have such as no pets, for example, and ensure the tenants fully understand them all.

Maintenance

You will begin to see your real estate passive income after the initial legwork is done, just like with everything else. When you have found the property you want, purchased it and found your tenants, you can then start to work out more clearly how you will receive the passive income from this investment.

If you have more experience in home maintenance, either through your own work at home or because you have experience with your other investment properties, you might actually take care of this yourself. You will need to have plumbers and electricians you can trust, however, as there are certain things that must be left to professionals. Make sure anybody you hire to work on the property is registered. It might also be worth your while to look for a reliable maintenance person who can take care of this for you. This will take some of the cash flow but will be a load off your mind.

You will start to see some cash flow i.e. passive income, after all expenses and any tax obligations have been taken care of each month. Anything left over will be yours to use in any way you wish. Using this particular passive income method is one of the most expensive to work with but it is also potentially one of the best cash flow acquisitions you can make once you begin to pay off your properties. The checks that will arrive each month are instant profit lines. When you become more experienced with property acquisition and rentals, your income from this will also likely grow and you can look forward to more time doing things you want to do.

Vacation Rentals
If you are a bit more adventurous you might want to look at vacation rentals. You will need to look up sites such as Airbnb. They describe themselves as *"a peer-to-peer online marketplace and homestay network enabling people to list or rent short-term lodging in residential properties, with the cost of such accommodation set by the property owner."*
There are more than one million listings on Airbnb around the world and around 60,000 guests. This online site connects travelers who are searching for vacation rentals.

If you decide to go the vacation rental passive income way then there are a few different options you can look at. You can sign up and become an Airbnb host. Since Airbnb is a trusted site where people can list and find unique accommodation pretty much anywhere in the world, this is an excellent site to use. Different price levels exist and Airbnb also has top-notch customer service with a steadily growing community of hosts and users.

You can find someone through Airbnb to use any extra space you might have and get some passive income that way, or if you have rental property you could use it/them as another option. You could list your rental property and you can do similar things as what you would do if you had a contracted tenant monthly or yearly. There are a few exceptions, however.

You could change a property into a bed and breakfast, for example. This would allow you to have multiple guests stay in the house and streamline even more profit. You get to meet people from different places around the world. You could choose a theme for each bedroom and market them individually.

If you choose to go the vacation rental option you have to have a plan for how you will manage and maintain the property. You could have a maintenance manager or do it yourself. A maintenance manager would be a good idea if you can afford one because this person would be available 24 hours for any odd jobs that need to be done. You could look into cleaning or housekeeping services, as the property will actually be like a small business. Every time a guest or guests leave the area it will need to be cleaned out and prepared for the new guests.

If you feel you can do things yourself then by all means do so but make sure things are done properly and done well. If your property isn't local and you live much further away it will likely be necessary to find a good real estate agent who will look after the property, keep keys and look after anything the guests need. All this will require money on a continual basis. Since Airbnb is based on customer satisfaction and reviews, you'll definitely need to keep up the maintenance and an excellent score so the property can continue to be booked and money can keep coming in.

CHAPTER 6: VARIOUS INCOME STREAMS

As you have seen there are so many potential avenues you can choose from which will allow for passive income to accumulate for you. Some might seem easier and more fun than others. In some cases there is more upfront work but there are also larger rewards. This is the good thing regarding passive income: once you've done the initial work you don't have to do too much later on. You can choose to work with one passive income stream or many; it's up to you.

If you begin with an easy stream you will be able to do it and it won't be an overwhelming task. It is very possible to achieve passive income but start with something you feel you can do at first and then you can move on to other more challenging aspects. The easiest passive income streams to start off with are Kindle and blogging.

Once you have successfully started some work you can save up a bit of extra money and keep it as an emergency fund. This could hold money that will be necessary to start your next business venture. If you are an individual who has debt then you could use this extra income to pay off your debts.

If you begin to feel more comfortable you might want to check out Amazon's FBA scheme and begin to explore the selling aspect. Real estate or Airbnb are more ambitious areas and will require bigger and more expensive investments. This doesn't mean they won't be a good source of passive income, but you will need more confidence and research and it is a longer-term goal you can move into slowly.

It is beneficial to put some effort into a few diverse active streams because no one can see what the future holds. If one stream dries up for whatever reason you will not be left without any income. With a few different income streams there is no fear of that happening. You've probably heard the saying, don't put all your eggs in one basket. When you have a few different streams going at once you should be earning more than what you're spending. You will be able to pay off any debts or properties and start making even more passive income.

The Potential is Unlimited
The potential to achieve your dreams in unlimited. At the beginning of this book what did you want to get out of it? Did you want to make some extra money on the side? Did you want to resign from a 9-5 job and have more time to spend with your family? Did you want to do something that would allow you to travel more?

Creating and maintaining a passive income will give you an opportunity to do all of those things and more. If the income streams you create for yourself work properly you'll have a lot of free time due to the passive income arriving in your bank account.

Passive income will give people the ability and time to do the things they wish they had some time for right now. Whether we like it or not, all of us need money. Most of us make it by working for someone else and earning it. We work hard and often long hours, many times in jobs we don't really like. Now that you have equipped yourself with the knowledge and tools to take a chance and start making the best of the skills and talents you have, you can have the life you desire. Every one of us was born with unique gifts. It is up to you to find them, figure out what you're good at and what makes you happy. Imagine doing what makes you happy and earning an easy living out of it! In this case, you could make a few livings from it.

Don't wait and don't procrastinate. This is the worst thing you can do. Give it a try. If you don't try you will never know. Waiting or procrastinating is just more missed income. If you decide to wait too long and let everything sink in you could be missing opportunities while John and Jane Doe next door have already started and have several different income streams already working for them. They are paying off their debts and have invested in property. Don't allow fear or laziness to stop you from going for your dreams. In order to succeed at something you must first give it a try. You can begin to build things. Do what works and continue to do it. If, for some reason, it stops working for you, do something else.

You must check in with yourself often. Ask yourself why you are doing something. Is it only for the money? Customers or audiences will pick up on this at some point and might perhaps look elsewhere for their goods or services. Your intentions are really what should move you in a certain direction. Be aware of what your intentions are. There's nothing wrong with making money. It's the way you do it that will make all the difference, however. You can focus on making money without it being the only thing you have in mind when doing what you do.

Continue building your own platform. Don't stop sharing the passion and the message you have, whether it is on podcasts, blogs or your own YouTube channels. You can't serve everybody but you can and should serve your target audience.

Whichever stream you choose for achieving financial freedom, remember, it won't always be straightforward but rather a meandering stream you must navigate. Use the skills you already have and make time to learn new skills as well for this will serve you in the future. Remain focused on the longer-term goals you have set for yourself in order to succeed and remember to believe in yourself and your vision.

THANKS FOR READING

We really hope you enjoyed this book. If you found this material helpful feel free to share it with friends. You can also help others find it by leaving a review where you purchased the book. Your feedback will help us continue to write books you love.

The Smart Reads library is growing by the day! Make sure and check out the other wonderful books in our catalog. We would love to hear which books are your favorite.

Visit:
www.smartreads.co/freebooks
to receive Smart Reads books for FREE

Check us out on Instagram:
www.instagram.com/smart_readers
@smart_readers

Don't forget your 2 FREE audiobooks.
Use this link www.audibletrial.com/Travis to claim
your 2 FREE Books.

SMART READS ORIGINS

Smart Reads was born out of the desire to find the best information fast without having to wade through the sheer volume of fluff available online. Smart Reads combs through massive amounts of knowledge compiles the best into quick to read books on a variety of subjects.

We consider ourselves Smart Readers, not dummies. We know reading is smart. We're self taught. We like to learn a TON about a WIDE variety of topics. We have developed a love for books and we find intelligence attractive.

We found that each new topic we tried to learn about started with the challenge of finding the pieces of the puzzle that mattered most. It can becomes treasure hunt rather than an education.

Smart Reads wants to find the best of the best information for you. To condense it into a package that you can consume in an hour or less. So you can read more books about more topics in less time.

OUR MISSION

Smart Reads aims to accelerate the availability of useful information and will publish a high quality book on every major topic on amazon.

Smart Reads hopes to remove barriers to sharing by taking the copyright off everything we publish and donating it to the public domain. We hope other publishers and authors will follow our example.

Our goal is to donate $1,000,000 or more by 2020 to build over 2,000 schools by giving 5% of our net profit to Pencils of Promise.

We want to Restore forests around the globe by planting a tree for every 10 physical books we sell and hope to plant over 100,000 trees by 2020.

Doesn't it feel good knowing that by educating yourself you are helping the world be a better place!? We think so too…

Thanks for helping us help the world. You Smart Reader you…

Travis and the Smart Reads Team

WHY I STARTED SMART READS

Every time I wanted to learn about something new I'd have to buy 20 books on the topic and spend way too long sorting through them and reading them all until I arrived at the big picture. Until I had enough perspectives to know who was just guessing, who was uninformed and who had stumbled upon something remarkable.

I wished someone else could just go in and figure that out for me and tell me what matters. That's how smart reads was born. I want smart reads to be a company that does all that research up front. Sorts through all the content that is available on each topic and pulls out the most up to date complete understanding, then have people smarter than me package the best wisdom in an easy to understand way in the least amount of words possible.

For example, I got a new puppy so I wanted to learn about dog training. I bought 14 different books about dog training and by the time I got through the first 5 and finally started getting the big picture on the best way to train my puppy she had grown up into a dog.

Yeah she's well behaved. She doesn't poop in the house. I can get her to sit and come when I call. But what if someone else went in and read all those books for me, found the underlying themes and picked out the best information that would give me the big picture and get me right to the point. And I'd only have to read one book instead of 15.

That would be amazing. I would save time. And maybe my dog would be rolling over, cleaning up after my kids and doing the dishes by now.That my friend, is the reason I started smart reads. Because I wanted a company I can trust to deliver me the best information in an easy to understand way that I can digest in under an hour. Because dog training is one of many subjects I want to master.

The quicker I can learn a wide variety of topics the sooner that information can begin playing a role in shaping my future. And none of us knows how long that future will be. So why not do everything we can to make the best of it and consume a ton of knowledge. And I figured all the better if I can also make a positive difference in the world.

That's why we're also building schools, planting trees and challenging ideas about copyright's place in today's world. Because as a company we have to be doing everything we can to support the ecosystem that gives us all these beautiful places to read our books. Thanks for reading.

Travis

Customers Who Bought This Book Also Bought

Success Principles: Techniques for Positive Thinking, Self-Love and Developing a Powerful Mindset

Understanding Affiliate Marketing: An Internet Marketing Guide for How To Make Money Online Using Products, Websites and Services

Credit Repair Guide: How to Fix Credit Score and Remove Negatives From Credit Report

Self-Esteem Supercharger: Build Self Worth and Find Your Inner Confidence

Develop Self-Discipline: Daily Habit to Make Self Confidence and Will Power Automatic